My Paper Children

Michele Heeney

My Paper Children

Michele Heeney

ARPress
ILLUMINATING IDEAS.
EMPOWERING VOICES

ARPress
45 Dan Road Suite 5
Canton MA 02021
Hotline: 1(888) 821-0229
Fax: 1(508) 545-7580

Ordering Information:

Quantity sales. Special discounts are available on quantity purchases by corporations, associations, and others. For details, contact the publisher at the address above.

Printed in the United States of America.

ISBN-13:	Softcover	979-8-89356-346-7
	Hardcover	979-8-89356-348-1
	eBook	979-8-89356-347-4

Library of Congress Control Number: 2024906331

Dedicated to Peggy's Vegetable Garden

Born of the creative, spiritual and magical part of my life.

They come out of my childhood in Western Pennsylvania and my life in California: San Francisco, during the sixties, then Marin and Monterey.

Many are from my 14 years as caretaker on 6000 acres of wilderness in Carmel Valley, just north of Big Sur, where I lived with my dog Honey.

Some came easy, and others took years to clean up and nurture.

A few poems are from time working in West Africa. A few out of the tradewinds of Maui, Hawaii. Others are from my deep love of Mexico and it's people.

A handful are from New Mexico, where I live on the Cochiti Reservation, near Santa Fe.

I am blessed with my children, none from my womb, and all from my heart.

Everyone has a life story. This is part of mine, as told by my poems and my photographs.

COCHITI LAKE

NEW MEXICO

2004-2007

The Most Beautiful Bird In The World

Could Be you.
An ethereal spirit-bird;
One wing of wisdom,
One of compassion.

You could fly
On the winds of pure kindness
Into the golden corona
Of the sacred sun.

But you will need
Both wings

THE GREAT SPIRIT

Chasing after little loves
I am road weary
And burning
In the driest desert
Tripping over
Sharp cactus
I stand with
Bloody legs,
A heart full
Of a gritty sort of silt.

When all the while
YOU were right here,
Succulent and sweet,
Lightly sitting on
My left breast.

DREAM Trails

The wind whips down the buffalo trail
As the dust blows thru my dreams
And in them I ride on a buffalo's back
As I wonder how real it all seems.

Where do they go, all these buffalo trails?
Off to a time that is gone?
To a place where all the buffalo herds
As the crow's flew above, grazed on.

Now, in my dream, I ride on a buffalo's back,
I can feel it's fur in my hands,
And I long for the peace of an innocent time
Thru the most enchanting of lands.

Much was lost along the buffalo trails.
Lost like the words to some song.
Yet, I see in my dream a large buffalo herd
And grieve for a past that is gone.

Shadow Side

Where is my deep poet?
The seeker of shadow,
The reader of dreams.

Where is my dark angel?
That watches at evening
As the blackbird sleeps.

Knows where the rabbits run
As the nitehawk hunts,
And how the river holds the moonlight.

Where is my secret self?
Who flashes gold spurs
In the chilly cool of dawn

Then gone!

MEXICO

Ongoing

To Run Alone

I am responsible of late,
Keeping needs and hopes behind a heavy gate,
Letting "Wondergirl" run wild about
Keeping pain and feelings out.

Once in a while my heart breaks through the ice
Of that cold, gray lake it's drowned in twice
And stings me with its hot reality
That you and your love are not here with me.

I run alone so well, it just seems right
To give my all on this long and solo flight.
But since you've touched me with your face
It seems now a sad and sorry race-

                                    To run alone.

Live Wire Fence

Had I only known one touch
Would send shots of lightening
Thru my bones and heart and skin
So sharp and deep, a bolt of raw electric

To scorch my body up and down
Singe my hair and upper lip
Burn holes in my socks and shoes
Searing thru the floor and into the cellar.

Had I only thought one touch
Could blind my eyes
So they could not see the present
Scorch my ears
So they could not hear the now
Leaving me stuck and staring at the past.

What once was calm and tranquil
Is burnt to ashes by the heat.
Yet after all this carnage,
I want another touch.

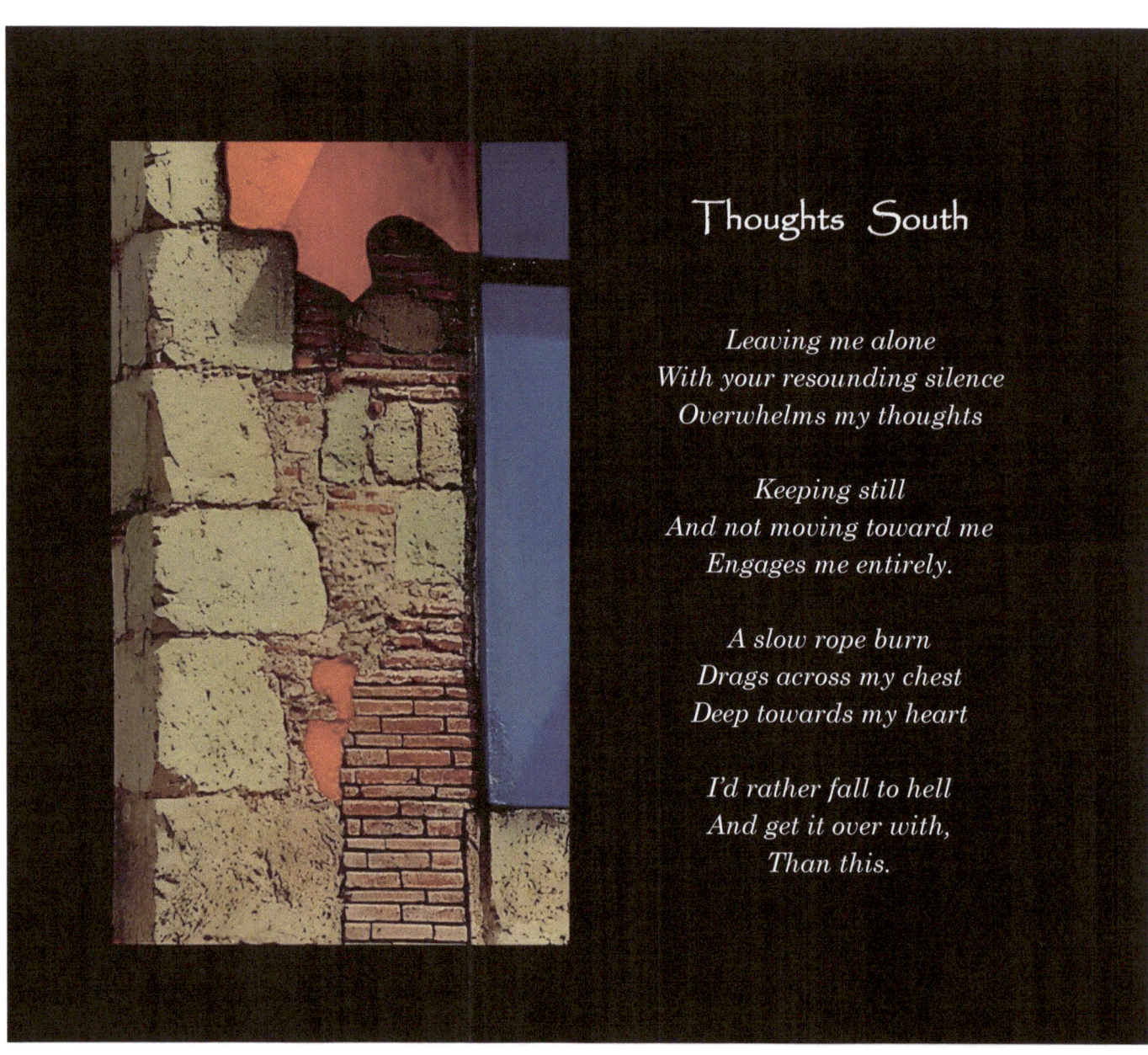

Thoughts South

Leaving me alone
With your resounding silence
Overwhelms my thoughts

Keeping still
And not moving toward me
Engages me entirely.

A slow rope burn
Drags across my chest
Deep towards my heart

I'd rather fall to hell
And get it over with,
Than this.

La Bebida Especial

When it comes to love,
    I often find
    A small sip of poison
    Is much more fine
    Than a big full glass
        Of the best red wine.

THE YEAR OF THE HORSE

Loving you was like
Riding a greased horse
Whose tail was soaked in oil
And braided with sticks of dynamite.
Each leg a different length.

Loving you was like riding this horse
Up a slippery hill
Into a winter ice storm.
With no saddle,
No bit between his teeth.

Then, one spark too many,
And we both exploded
Into bright pieces and bits-
Much like the stars-
Across the night sky.

MEXICO

Mexico. Sweet Mexico
Your sunsets glow,
Your colors flow,
Your warm winds blow.

Now, all I want to do
Is go
To Mexico.

I hear the whisper
Of the brown Madonna's song
The music of fiestas wafts along.
I love your high Sierra Madre
Your salty, sensual sea.

Please, Mexico
Save a little place for me.

CARMEL VALLEY
CALIFORNIA

1991-2004

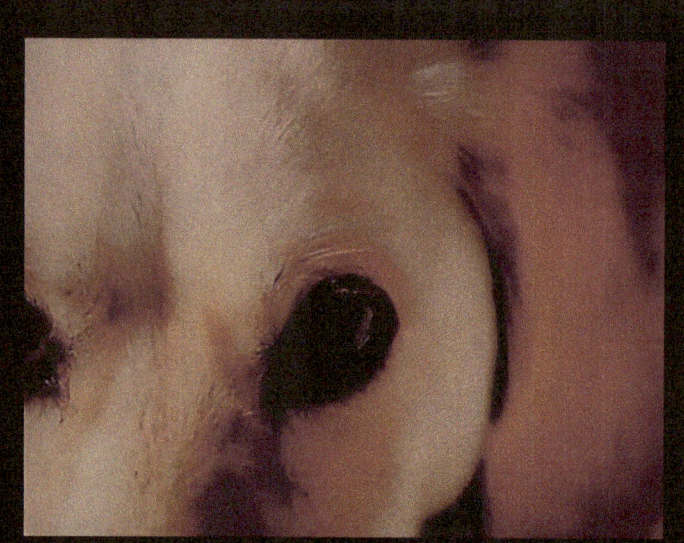

My Dog Honey

Honey went to heaven
In a bright blue boat
Honey went to heaven
Didn't leave a note

Can't quite believe it
That she'd up and leave it
Honey went to heaven
In a boat.

Honey went to heaven
In a pickup truck
Flying down the highway
When the brake got stuck

Honey went to heaven
And I'm still here
Honey went to heaven
Gone for good I fear

Honey went to heaven,
And left me here

Star & Stripes

The prince rode in
With a golden lance.
He yearned for power,
He took his chance.
He stole the crown.

 He suffered a wound
 As he walked the hall
 On the marbled floor
 Of the castle tall.
 And so he bled.

  All his knights sent out
  With armor bright,
  Along the borders,
  Prepared to fight.
  And so they stood..

   The land grew cold,
   The crops grew dry.
   Long shadows fell
   Over earth and sky.
    The wide world changed.

Now, like Parsifal,
A young man comes
Up to the castle
And chants and drums,
 "What ails you, Prince,
 What ails you?"

The Hummingbirds

To all who've never
Lived in Middleworld
That space somewhere
Between heaven and earth

To all the strong and sturdy ones
Not choked by an army of a
Thousand colored billboards
Strangled by a tangle of a million
New cemented freeways
Crushed by each evil, insane
Trumped-up war

I salute you!

But don't tramp down on us
So heavily
Don't brush the feather covered
Ones away, the hummingbirds.

We have a certain strength,
Even though it may seem waning
With each new decade.
You may be losing much
By losing us.

18

Garland Summer

Heartbreakable star-drenched sky
Velvet black in deep July,
My blood turns to honey wine
Warmed by the breath
Of ocean winds that drift
Through tall and flaxen wheat
On waves of summer heat.

Our skin turns pink, then peach, then tan
And sweet apricot juice stains
My shirt and hand
While your hair is blown about
Like wild cornsilk in the breeze.

Sweet July and August
Run together, and soon
We feel as young as
Any yearling doe under the moon
Grazing on fallen
Plums at night

All but forgotten
Cold February's chill
Month of brittle bones
And frozen dawns
Without the bright orange sun's goodwill.

Stay! Oh warm July
And linger long.
Too soon comes the gray
Of winter crushing wheel
When blood turns again to blood
And bones to steel.

AT ESALEN

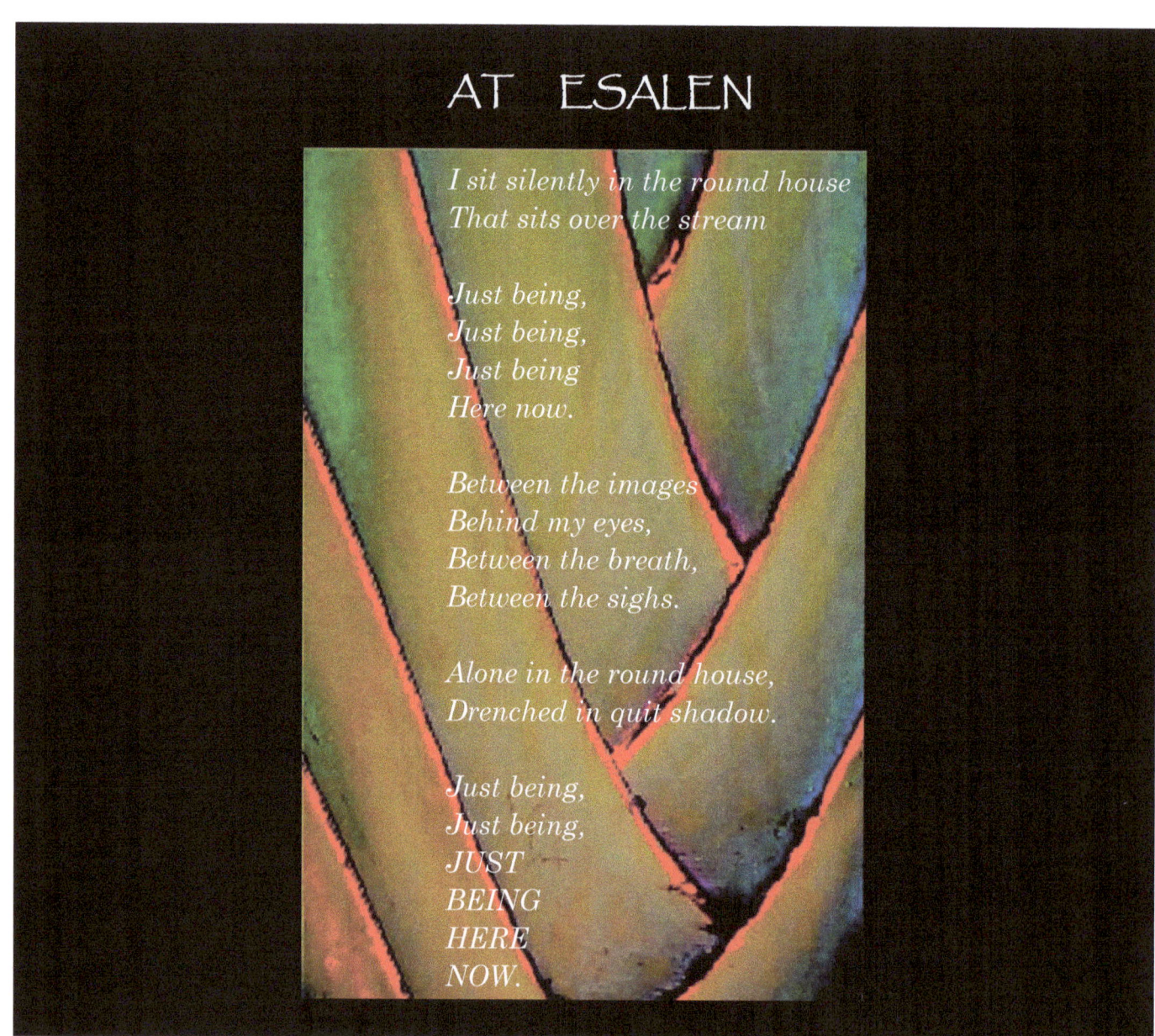

I sit silently in the round house
That sits over the stream

Just being,
Just being,
Just being
Here now.

Between the images
Behind my eyes,
Between the breath,
Between the sighs.

Alone in the round house,
Drenched in quit shadow.

Just being,
Just being,
JUST
BEING
HERE
NOW.

MY LIFE

My life
Sometimes takes off
Without me.
Lurching forward
When I'm sure
I had it in reverse.

My life
Takes sharp curves
Before I ever
Put the key in.
Smashes into trees,
And knocks down fences.

I've often felt
I wasn't at the wheel
At all.
Just pulled along
By some old rope
Scrapped up from knees to chin.

Up another hill?
When I thought
It's time to get some rest.
Out for a cruise?
When I thought,
I should be in bed

God no.
Not another freeway.
Can't we just try
A quiet country road
Oh well,
At least
Let me get my hat.

The Santa Cruz Detox Diet Blues

To get these pesky toxins out
We eat a lot of greens
We eat a lot of fiber too
To get our insides clean.

We chomp on celery, grains and fruit
Avoiding meat and dairy
And when it comes to sweets, my dear
We must be truly wary.

Lots of water is the rule
And processed foods are out
Whole foods are always best for us
And veggies hold some major clout.

Please don't forget your protein drink
To keep your courage strong
Because this culinary trip
Will be just three weeks long.

CRAZY LOVE

Lightly Walks Alone
Met Tramps Down With Thunder
Oh, what a mess
Oh, what a blunder!

But wasn't it a joy
And wasn't it a wonder
When Lightly Walks Alone
Loved Tramps Down With Thunder.

LAS SALINAS LATINAS

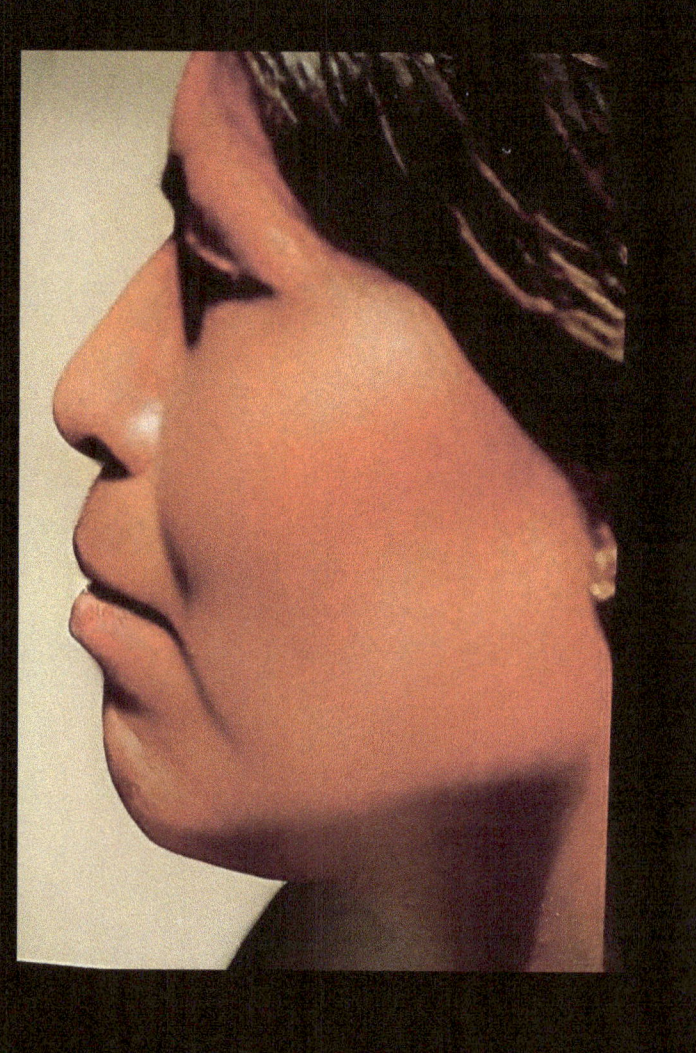

All those lovely Mexicans
Round, brown and sweet.
Full of heart and gentleness
They helped me to my feet.

Helped me find my way again,
Helped with so much more.
All those lovely Mexicans,
I love them to the core.

The Scream

A sharp red silver
Of a long high scream
Cut the black silk night
To ribbons

With that, I knew
The night and the scream
Were mine
Black silk ribbons

And all

A Dream of my Muse

Sky music woman
Into the night
Thru starstreams and moon dreams
On a heavenly flight.

Stay angel lady
Don't fly away
Teach me your soul songs
In the music you play.

Whisper wind sonnets
While flying so high
Over the ocean
Straight into the sky.

Where are you off to?
Your thoughts are your own.
I should have guessed it,
You're flying us home.

Sweet September sings a haunting song
Of chilly days and frosted nights
And yet she gaily goes along
In her resplendent robes
Of red and golden lights.

Summer's past her peak
But still she charms
With all the force
Of her adolescent ways
Along the meadows and the farms
Filled high with harvest
Where all the season's treasures lay.

Yet September
Hums an ancient tune
That tells of fear and dread
Beneath her autumn sky
Of bright stars
And harvest moon,
She has a dagger hidden
In her glowing gown of red.

She shivers hard and long
Causing cold bones
And nights to splinter
She shutters with a chill so strong
For she knows

That all too soon
She'll have to sleep
With winter.

September

Monterey Days

The teacher is effective
Who is always learning
Keeping an ear for the unknown
So the known is easier shared.

The position is delicate,
The scales easily shift.
But having knowledge of the weights,
One understands the balance.

Standing in Front of Your Door

I once had a blood red heart
It sang
It soared
It cried.

Now it's stuck
To the sole
Of your shoe.

Now there's a hole
In my chest
Where my heart used to be.

And it's cold
It's sad
And it's empty.

And I'm here
At your doorstep
To say
I want my heart back.

Fool Moon

This big full moon
Takes a hold of me
Won't set me free
Till the end of night.

That bright orb hanging
Keeps my brains a clanging
Gets strange ghosts a banging
Like some old barn doors.

This big full moon
With it's neon grin
Takes me by the throat
Brings the night witch in.

This cool moon glow
With it's ice blue light
Takes a hold of me
Till the end of night

Till the dawn.

Celibacy

When I knew for certain
That no man would soon be near,
I took the angels on.

And in that coupling
My heart blew open.
And beauty,
That had been
A stranger to me,

Poured forth
Like golden water falls.

La Loba

I am a wolf
Wild, sleek and grey,
I hunt by nite
I sleep by day.

No one can catch me
No one's as swift.
From one hill to another
I silently shift.

You may see me at dawn
At daybreaks first light,
A flash of wilderness,
I'm a dazzling sight.

There's dew on my coat
Mud on my paws
Blood on my mouth
And meat in my jaws.

I am a wolf
Wild, sleek and grey
I hunt by nite
I sleep by day.

To the Blue Crane
at Garland Ranch

Blue Crane
Sees me,
I see him.

Marsh reeds
Long stems
Finds an artful way

For the Blue Crane
To blend with
An early fog filled day.

Yet, the Blue Crane
Sees me
And I see him.

The Photograph

I've got your image
Caught it in a box,
From a fleeting moment-
I'm a crafty fox.

Off to the darkroom,
Such a magic place
Out pops the moment
Out pops your face.

Up from the pan!
Out to the light!
Now I've got you.
Got you just right.

A Drunken Dragonfly

I am the deep black ink
That keeps the stars afloat.
I am the endless cosmic night.

I am the life force of every living thing.
I am your blood, your secret heart, your soul.
I am where your spirit goes at death.

I am that which measures wisdom and compassion,
And to whom all great religions call,
Though they've yet to speak My language well.

I write the music of the spheres
And teach the birds to sing it.
I am your prayers answered.

And still, you do not know Me.
Won't catch My name on solar winds,
Or hear My voice in ocean waves.

You're like a drunken dragonfly
That rips his wings off
While in the midst of flight.

WAKE UP!
You're missing quite a show.

MAUI
HAWAII

1988–1991

KONA TURTLES

All those flights
Across the airways
All that rattling around in bed.
And have we touched yet?

Candy kisses left in my shoe
Then you're off again,
Leaves me a little lost.
And have we loved yet?

All the hellos, goodbyes,
Too long in coming,
Too soon in going.
And have we met yet?

While all I really want to know
Is where you keep your feelings,
In that turtle shell of yours.
And have you been there?

TIDES AND TRADEWINDS

Ocean music.
Echoes of time
Beyond our beginning.

Flowing out
Toward eternity
And back again.

While on the soft four winds
Floats the fragrance
Of a thousand different blooms.

Back
To
California

1973-1955

TIME

Willowy aftermath
Of half remembered dreams.

Gossamer mist dividing
Today from forever.

We watch our hours
From a door beyond,

And pass thru
In silken slippers.

The Dancer

A novelette of delicacy,
A living poem
Of contradictions,
Of dreams and coarse reality,
A sideshow of a sideshow,
Yet all the while
The main event.

A study of agony,
The master of ecstasy,
With a palette of joy
A canvas of heartache.
Having sung Gregorian in Heaven
And danced as passionately in Hell
Almost as often,
Enjoying both-
Equally.

Drinking the beer,
Singing the songs,
Laughing, breathing, living,
All, all with the eye of an artist
Splashes of oil paint
All over her dress.

The clown of a million sighs,
The leprechaun of a thousand words,
Knee deep in life
Yet far above the curtained stage.

Disenchanted with the world
Of too, too many trumpets
Crescendos on to high a pitch,
Yet gaily marching with the crowd.

To An Old Love

Oh what a masquerade I played
To pleasure you!
You left anyway.

I simply could have
Been myself.
Then at least-
You would be leaving
Me.

Love Song

A flutter of emotion,
Then sudden flight
On frantic wings.

Freed,
From a twice-locked cage
My hopes went flying

To sing silent notes of need
Upon your windowsill.

Liberia
West Africa

1972 ~ 1973

Liberia

All those beautiful
Black woman
In their flowing
Colored skirts
And tall headwraps
Of the same bright cloth,
Swaying along like palm trees,
Carrying fruit and rice
On their heads
In huge enamel bowls

I soon came to feel
Quite ridiculous
With my white legs
Sticking out
Carrying a purse I'd bought
In San Francisco.

LIBERIA: before the war

I remember sitting on the front porch
Of a friends house in West Africa
Looking at the moon
Falling in love with it's face
As though it were something
I'd seen just then, for the first time

I remember the night
For its huge stillness
Its quieting heat
Black figures walking slowly
Down the dirt road
Murmuring to one another,
And wondering, I suppose,
What we were doing in their small village.

I remember the next morning we got up
To eat some bananas and sugar cane
And visit with a family
Who lived some miles outside the town.

I remember and wonder now
Was there really such a place
Of such exquisite peace.
Of such perfect sweetness.

African Gentleman

We were walking along the beach
To the small Town near our little house
In Fishtown, on the Atlantic.
I was trudging far behind
When a Kru fisherman, quite tall
Appeared from the bush.
He was wrapped in a long
Blue cloth of cotton
Against his dark brown skin.
He spoke no English,
But took my large pack
To carry for me.
We walked along the sea for hours
He cut a coconut for us to drink.
When we reached the river,
Just before the town,
He rowed us across.
When I waved goodbye
He picked up a small seashell
And gave it to me
As a parting gift.

WEST AFRICAN EBONY

Never knowing
What sweet bits of our hearts
Were caught in the dust
Of their brooms

People came with feather dusters
And brooms of black and white
To whisk away all of the space
And most of the time,
Then left.

Just as I was thinking
We had a good chance
Of reaching out
To explore each others face
But that takes time
And plenty of space.

THE GIFT

It was a short, but touching romance.
You came in one day
Tall and gleaming black
We played some card games,
And you told my fortune.
We were drinking whiskey
And laughing a lot.

I showed you my pictures from home.
You told me about Alabama.
You picked me up and carried me
To my small bed
Where we covered ourselves
With each other's sweat.
It was such a hot African night

After delicious hours
We walked to a store
And drank a couple sodas.

Weeks later, you gave me a pin
You'd bought in Ivory Coast,
A lady carved of ivory.

Now, all these thousands of miles away
I feel just like that lady
Carved of ivory
Who sits in my jewelry box.

San Francisco

AND

MARIN COUNTY

1968 ~ 1988

Mt. Tamalpais

Weary of wishing
Soft lay me down,
Spent of ambition,
On your cool ground.

High mother mountain,
On thee I rest.
Peace from your fountain
I drink from your breast.

Cradle me sweetly
As I sleep by your streams,
Humbly I seek thee,
To nourish old dreams.

Eduardo

When you've finally tired
Of tasting all the silver fruit
When you've caught
All the golden fish
The seas can hold
Picked every summer flower

When at last
The cup is emptied
The searching done
And you pause,
Remember one lone heart
That truly loved you.
Recall that one soul
Touched your fleeting soul
And shared the presence
Of a certain peace.

Earth Walk

I used to walk with angels
An infinity ago,
In a land of yellow butterflies
Pink dreams as light as snow.

But darling you woke the dreamer
I'll not be the same again
And it seems much more like living
To walk in the world of men.

I Ching Days

Time enough
For all things
We need to know.
Take time to savor
Every living day.

All is known
At any one moment
And there is
Only one now.

So quiet the many,
Accept the multilevels.
No need for conflict
Space abounds within.

The varied forces
Suspend themselves
In perfect alignment,
Simply allow them.

California Goodbye

We've filled our basket with roses,
With bits of dark autumn moss
Bright beads of dew from spring time
Last winter's delicate frost.

We've fastioned coats of velvet
To wrap us from the wind,
Bought sweet wine from far off places,
Crystal glasses to pour it in.

We've waded thru silken rivers
With fish carved of amethyst
Tied ribbons of rainbow around our waist
Wove threads of gold wheat for our wrist.

Though my heart is filled high with sorrow
I'm letting go of your hand
For I'm off to another beginning
And I'm praying you'll understand.

3 Short Poems

I wrote on my grocery list today:
A bunch of spinach
A pound of butter
A carton of milk
A little peace of mind.

What Do Women Want

When I finally made you buy
Me a birthday present
Didn't you know
I wanted
A necklace of stardust
Not a bracelet of gold?

After all the traumas
I decided to love you.
You seemed so safe.

I soon discovered
There is no safety
With or without you

And nothing so silly
As deciding to fall in love.

Where Are They

I'm often quite amazed
At the total lack of
Handsome men
Waiting at my doorstep
While I'm sitting
On my moonlit porch
In the shadows of tall redwoods
Feeling quite high
And very beautiful.

TOMORROW

We are day-eaters-all.
Gluttons of time.
Mindlessly taking in
Morsels of moments
That will be served
But once.

Tomorrow we'll drink a bitter brew
Of sad regrets
To clear our mouths and minds
Of our half-tasted yesterdays.

Fairfax Summer

I'm lying in the sun
Hot, sweating,
Greasy from oil,
Warm skin,
Slippery legs and arms,
Drowsy and lazy.

Wish you'd come along
And slide all over me.

The Big Question

What will you be
When you come to me
Into my garden?

A fine large tree
With big green leaves
To comfort me?

A bird
Whose song is light
That comes to sing to me at night?

A butterfly
That flies about
Bringing little children out?

A summer stream
That cools the heat,
And flows across
My toes and feet?
Flowers that dot my eyes
Or puffy skies?

Or a FENCE that goes around
And up and down
To tell me where to go
And what to know
In my very own
And rather nice
Private meadow?

Eduardo

Colors I thought I'd left behind
Now seep like melted wax
Across the canvas of my mind.

Splashes of red and blue
Streams of yellow and pink
Run like rivers
Over my landscape.

Rainbows again
Out of the grey
Boxes of crayons
To color my day.

Don't take your brushes away
Or put the paints on a shelf,
Fill in a few more spaces for me
With the colors you've made for yourself.

Today was Memorial Day.
I wasn't invited to any picnics.
I did, however, have some fun.
Rode my bike up white's Hill
Hot, tired, face beating,
Flying down the other side
Calling out Sweet Jesus
All that cool wind in my hair.

I stopped and had a pepsi
In front of a little store in Forest Knolls
To watch all the lovers
Off to picnics in wild Olema.

Back on the bike again
Blowing down the hill again,
Rear end up,
Shoulders down,
Thinking-
Thank God for Memorial Day!

THE MISSING PIANO

If only I had learned to play
I know I could have been
A stellar pianist,
With a fantastic feel for the music
An unearthly depth of spirit
A religious feel for the art.
Strewing stained glass soul bubbles everywhere.

Instead, I scratch on papers
Pretty words from my heart.

SWEET AND SOUR

Alone again
Alone at last!
Alone again
Alone, alas.

Christmas

Christmas comes but once a year
I think that's rather nice
Because the good lord only knows
I couldn't take it twice.

Zen, Again

We are always
At the present moment
The sum total
Of all our past decisions
And all our future dreams.

Ah, not so
Says the stranger.
We are always the sum total
Of that quit being
Who always lives in the presence
Of the ever present now.

A Short Summation

Ten small holes
And that's about
Enough to let it all in
And let it all out.

Outside My Window

They all worked well
Like little bees
Some on the ground
Some up the tress,

When they were done
A joyful thing!
From the big oak branch
Hung a brand new swing.

Carey

Waiting puts me in a box
Waiting makes my stomach churn.
I keep looking up from the morning dishes
Expecting to see
Your face.

FALLEN PETALS

I'm a special breed of rose

Hold me too close

And I'll wither

Not close enough

And I'll die.

WESTERN PENNSYLVANIA

1946~1968

Vigil Lights

There were a few old fires
That have finally burnt out.
A few long time red hot embers
That have slowly expired,
Unnamed and smoldering longings
That flickered sporadically
Then died.

With all these beautiful bonfires
No longer raging
Soft and gentle lights
Now have been lit,
I stand before myself
Hypnotized by these
Crimson vigil lamps,
Worshipping their peaceful glow,
Dropping tokens of invisible alms
Into an imaginary box
In hopes you'll
Keep them lit for me.

The Holy Spirit

I am the house of fire,
And on I'll burn
As I do now—
Forever blazing.

I'm not the owner
Of this flame,
I am but the space
For its existence.

Not bleed
Flows through my veins,
But fire.
That fire alone can cool,
And yours alone.

TWO THIEVES

Age steals youth away,
Death steals more.
Age dusts the windows,
Death shuts the door.

Age takes beauty,
Death, hope of spring.
Age takes laughter,
Death—everything.

Age steals thoughts away
And times once known.
Age takes memories,
Death leaves its own.

Age knows good times
Death knows none.
Age takes many,
Death—everyone.

NIGHT FLIGHT

My heart, where will you go tonight,
Where will the soft wind take you?
Where is the end of your lonely flight,
Back to the dreams that will break you?

Stay, my heart. This I implore.
Oh must you go a-flying?
For when you leave to muse once more,
Here must I stay a-dying.

Take thee then, to the dreams so dead,
But when you return here tomorrow,
Expect me not a tear to shed,
When you come home-sick with sorrow.

Spring Conversation

I saw it, I did
I wouldn't lie.
I heard it was dead.
But I saw it fly.
You must be mistaken
And I'm quite sure it was dead.

All right then
Come with me
Over this hill
And under that tree
There the two
Saw a wonderful thing,
A tiny butterfly
Take to wing.

Aries

What drum is beating
After the long grey quiet
After the numb blank night?
What red vivid burst
Of surging force
Can still be beating?
After the sorrow
After the face to face meeting
With the low sad
Song of life?

What drum is beating?
MINE!

Wild Horses

Where are all the wild hot stallions
That sped across my landscape?
With flashing hooves and blood red eyes,
With steaming flesh and panting breath,
They tore through tender land,
Kicked up soul and sinew.

Led by one young white one,
Passion was his name
Passion was his life, and Freedom followed at his neck
Across my fresh green earth.
So wild and huge and free they ran,
With many more behind them.
Through white of day and blue of night,
Up hills of wonder, down valleys of regret.
They stopped for none, nor knew a master.

Now, I only hear their echo,
Feel but the last of shaking earth.
They're all but gone now.
Riding toward another golden sun,
Another promised land.
And I must stay,
To taste the dust of mine.

Last Poem To My First Love

So much wanting
And so much waiting
So much longing
And so much aching
Have finally taken
Their toll.

No longer I wait
For the touch that healed
For the voice
That warmed and cheered
I've prayed so hard
And waited so long
The need has now disappeared.

So I'm letting go dear,
Letting you go with regret.
I may never stop loving
But at last
I begin to forget.

PENNSYLVANIA WINTER

Clear, crisp air,
Pure soft snow.

High on wind whipped hills,
I look through ice cold glass

Into the winter's face,
Into the blue-black night,

With glittering moonglow
Through the window's frost,

And dream of all my winters gone,
And all my winters yet to come.

Home Remembered

Memories of green fields and oak trees
Bumble bees and honey suckle
Sunflowers, gold and high
With stalks of bristled down
Birds that sing on crystal mornings
Gently waking peaceful minds
Sidewalks with a million cracks
Morning glories that crawl thru fences
And run up and down dirt piles
With a hundred secret places
Elderberries, broken glass, lucky stones
In shades of white
Ant hills with little holes on top
Old men with canes who smile
Plants with bugs, big iron gates
Violets that grow in patches
Roses that grow with thorns
Happiness that seems to glisten
Warm sweaters when the world is cold
School days, puppy dogs and lizards
Soap that comes in little sizes
Socks of red and green and pink
Candy, paper boats and bubbles

Memories so fresh and green.
These are the teardrops of my childhood,
Gone like fairy tents at noon.

Friends

In your house
You were a stranger.
In mine, I was a stranger too,
O side by side
We came together
As strangers sometimes do.
Now, thru time and space forever,
We make a tribe of two.

Stair Steps

The end?

Another beginning?

Actually an unbroken line

Reaching out into infinity

Twisting into a spiral

Contorting into a staircase

That begins and ends upon itself.

How many more faces to love

To say goodbye?

Hardly matters anymore.

My face always

Stays the same,

Hasn't changed much

No matter how many

Hellos and goodbyes
It's managed to say.

THE CHILL

Then there was that morning
I awoke and was content

I no longer need to think high thoughts
Or even think at all.
All is good enough
I needn't change a thing.
Everything in grey shades
No longer black and white
I find no red rage
But blue complacency.
All is still and understandable.
My soul has stopped vibrating
My mind has stopped knowing
At my soul.

Ever since that dark cold morning
I long for discontent.

POSSESSED

Dark Heart
Why do you live in darkness
While all around is light?

Why must you look at sorrow
And take her for your own?
Don't you see in wasting beauty
You've wasted joy.

You create your pains
Then daily feed them
You nurture them with care.

You build your life
With rotting wood
And when you see the rot
You only build the more.

And in that dark strange
Place you've made,
The devil found his own.

ACKNOWLEDGMENT

I want to thank the following for their support:

Carolyn Stammely-Hutchinson
Peggy Williams
Mary Lausten
Pat Kachmar-Costlow
Nancy Abildgaard
Honey
Todd Black especially, for his design & technical skills

All the folks in my life who have brought
me my lessons, thru pain or kindness or both.

And, of course, the stunning geography of this dazzling azure planet of ours.
May we bless and keep her that way.